48646670R00111

Made in the USA
Columbia, SC
10 January 2019